THE DIRECTORY OF AUTOCEPHALOUS BISHOPS OF THE APOSTOLIC SUCCESSION
✝

THE DIRECTORY OF AUTOCEPHALOUS BISHOPS OF THE APOSTOLIC SUCCESSION

†

FIFTEENTH EDITION
REVISED AND EXPANDED

Edited by

Bishop Karl Prüter

A St. Willibrord's Press Book

THE BORGO PRESS
An Imprint of Wildside Press

MMVII

The Autocephalous Orthodox Churches
ISSN 1059-1001
Number One

FIFTEENTH EDITION

CONTENTS
†

PREFACE TO THE
FIFTEENTH EDITION
†

Greetings to all the bishops and servants of Jesus Christ from Karl Prüter.

I am happy to greet you and bring Fifteenth Edition of the *Directory of Autocephalous Bishops of the Apostolic Succession*. While our staff is working hard to insure the accuracy of each edition we need your help. As you know, that with your help, we prepared fourteen editions and we thank you. This edition will be larger and we need your continued support. As in previous editions we included a list of bishops with whom we have lost contact. Included in this Directory are bishops whom have you called to our attention when we published last year's Directory. We thank you and ask once again for your help.

Under the alphabetical listing of each bishop we have put the name of the jurisdiction he serves. Where we do not know, or are uncertain, we have omitted the jurisdictional name. I hope our readers will help us again and supply the missing data. Last year we started to add the names of Old Catholic and Orthodox bishops from all countries. This year we have added many more.

We do not list the prelate's phone number or e-mail address unless he requests that we do. Our years of experience have made us aware that the day the Directory comes off the press someone will have moved. In hopes that this may be avoided please contact us if you have a new address or a change of jurisdiction.

You may contact us at (417) 823-9902. Our address is 2835 South Fort Avenue, Apt. 1207, Springfield, Missouri 65807.

In Christ's Service,

†Karl Prüter
2007

THE DIRECTORY OF AUTOCEPHALOUS BISHOPS OF THE APOSTOLIC SUCCESSION
✝

Directory of Autocephalous Bishops

-A-

The Most Rev. Thomas Abel
Old Roman Catholic Church
Diocese of San Diego
2020 Chestnut Avenue
Carlsbad, CA 92008

The Most Rev. Michael Adams
Catholic Apostolic Church of Antioch
1003 East Madison
Fairfield, IA 52556
e-mail michael@adamsfamily.com

The Most Rev. Merrill Adamson
100 Delano Avenue
San Francisco, CA 94112

The Most Rev. Randolph Adler
Charismatic Episcopal Church
107 Marquita
San Clemente, CA 92672

The Most Rev. Aftimos II
4696 South East Horseshoe Court
Salem, Oregon 97301

The Most Rev. Theophilus J. Alcantara
316 Park Place
Brooklyn, New York 11238

The Most Rev. Aleksander
The Belarusian Autocephalous Orthodox
  Church
19 River Road
Highland Park, NJ 08904

The Rt. Rev. C. Ramon Allee
Community of St. James the Just Orthodox
  Church
P O. Box 92497
Long Beach, CA 90809-24297

The Most Rev. Joseph N. Allee
3918 Rosaliud Ave.
Chattanooga, TN 37416-3226

The Most Rev. John M. Allen
Anglican Catholic Church
Bull Run Road
Dravosberg, PA 15034

Directory of Autocephalous Bishops

The Most Rev. Robert J. Allmen
Reformed Catholic Church
P. O. Box 725
Hampton Bays, NY 11946
(631) 728-2633
Frboballmen@optonline.net

The Most Rev. Alfredo Alonso
National Catholic Apostolic Church
508 West 166th Street, Ste. 4-G
New York, NY 10032
(212) 568-5615

The Most Rev. Andreas
Ukrainian Orthodox Church
1117 Fraser Street
Bay City, MI 48708

The Rt. Rev. Andrew
American Orthodox Catholic Church
2335 Williamson Road
Saginaw, MI 48601

The Rt. Rev. Acie Angel
Christ Catholic Church International
1085 Wiethaupt Road
Florissant, MO 63031

The Rt. Rev. Eusbio E. Angulo
The American Catholic Orthodox Mission
241-54th Street
Hialeah, FL 33013

The Most Rev. Vernon Ashe
Mar Thomas Orthodox Church Outside of In-
dia
1133 East Olive Avenue
Fresno, CA 93728

-B-

The Rt. Rev. Ronald L. Bair
Free Anglican Church in America and The
  British Isles
P.O. Box 2436
West Palm Beach, Florida 33402

The Rt. Rev. Jeffrey Barberio
The Anglican Rite Jurisdiction in the Ameri-
  cas
P.O. Box 1974
Bloomfield, NJ 07003

The Most Rev. Karl J. Barwin
The Evangelical Catholic Church
P. O. Box 28624
Scottsdale, Arizona 85252-8907

The Most Rev. Craig W. Bates
Charismatic Episcopal Church
50 St. Thomas Place
Malverne, NY 11565

The Most Rev. Louis Battaglio
Brothers of Christ
6709 Stardust
North Lauderdale, FL 33068

The Most Rev. Theodore Bessette
National Catholic Apostolic Church
P.O. Box 157
Scott, Arkansas, 72142-0157
(501) 961-1482

The Most Rev. Rex Bartholomew Blasin-
   game
National Catholic Apostolic Church
22 Pear Street
Cabot, Arkansas 72023
(501) 843-7978

The Most Rev. Paul Bradley
Catholic Church of Christ
5567 East 97th Place
Thornton, CO 80229
(720) 366-3300
Cbrad99@aol.com

Directory of Autocephalous Bishops

The Rt. Rev. Brian E. Brown
Ecumenical Free Catholic Communion
6146 S. Farm Road 175
Ozark, MO 65721
(417) 598-0852
brian@free-catholic.org

The Rt. Rev. John Brown
Christ Catholic Church International
1504-75 Queen Street North
Hamilton, Ontario L9R 3J3
Canada

The Most Rev David R. Brown
American Orthodox Church
20043 Highway 36
Covington, LA 70433
(985) 893-3575

The Most Rev. Randolph A. Brown
The Western Orthodox Church in America
5917-73rd Avenue North, #4
Brooklyn Park, MN 55429-1100
(763) 232-8939
bpbrown@comcast.net

The Most Rev. Jack Brownwell
1416 Parkview Avenue
San Jose, CA 93130

The Most Rev. Brian Burch
Old Roman Catholic church in Canada
20 Spruce Street
Toronto, Ontario M5A 2H7
(416) 969-8794
burch@web.com

The Most Rev. George Burke
Life of Christ Monastery
1482 Rango Way
Borrego Springs, CA 92004

The Rt. Rev. Robert J. Burke
Apostolic National Catholic Church
262 Peat Meadow Road
New Haven, CT 06513

The Most Rev. William H. Bushnell
Old Holy Catholic Church
728 Briarcliff Lane South
Madison Heights, VA 24572-6039
(434) 384-0549

The Rt. Rev. Jamen Butler
The African Orthodox Church
1533 North 57th Street
Philadelphia, PA 19131

Directory of Autocephalous Bishops

The Most Rev. Donald J. Buttenbusch
National Catholic Apostolic Church
2502 Cottman Avenue
Philadelphia, PA 19135-1107
(215) 332-2831

-C-

The Rt. Rev. Reuben Cabigting
The Liberal Catholic Church
P.O. Box 270
Wheaton, Illinois 60189

The Most Rev. Patrick J. Callahan
Ecumenical Catholic Church
1601 Acorn Court
Yorba Linda, CA 92686

The Rt. Rev. Robert J. Calof
Free Anglican Church in America and The
   British Isles
23209 Berendo
Harbor City, CA 90710

The Most Rev. Lawrence M. Cameron
United Catholic Church
1668 Sylvania Avenue
Toledo, OH 53612

Directory of Autocephalous Bishops

The Most Rev. Brian Carsten
Orthodox Catholic Church of America
5355 County Road 35
Auburn, IN 46706-9717
Ebe7695@aol.com

The Rt. Rev. Richard Castle
3533 Loloff Road
Quesnel, British Columbia V2J 6E5
Canada

The Most Rev. William Champion
Anglican Rite Old Catholic Church
P. O. Box 924944
Houston, Texas 77292-4944

The Most Rev. Armand Chorwinard
Western Orthodox Church of America
P.O. Box 1412
Lodi, CA 95241-1412

The Most Rev. William L. Christen
United Catholic Church
3060 W. Belle Avenue
Queen Creek, AZ 85242

The Most Rev. Thomas C. Clary
Free Catholic Church
3510 Front Street, Suite 1F
San Diego, CA 92103
tccdiego@aol.com

The Most Rev. Paul M. Clement
Catholic Apostolic Church of Antioch-
  Malabar Rite
13386 North Bloomfield Road
Nevada City, CA 95959

The Most Rev. Robert M. Clement
American Catholic Church
414 New Hampshire Drive
Los Angeles, CA 90027
(323) 668-0008

The Most Rev. Paul H. Combs
Old Catholic Church of North America
P.O. Box 260473
Tampa, Florida 33685
Phone (873) 963-7099
e-mail amcath@aol.com

Directory of Autocephalous Bishops

The Most Rev. Donald Connell
Christ the King Covenant Church
P. O. Box 909
Weatherford, Texas 76086
(817) 594-8720
ckcc_main@sbcglobal.net

The Most Rev. William E. Conner
The Independent Episcopal Church
P. O. Box 140182
Dallas, Texas 75214
Phone: (972) 900-7298

The Most Rev. Constantine
One Holy Catholic and Apostolic Orthodox
   Church
340 NE 18th Ave., Suite 2-103
Homestead, Florida 33033

The Most Rev. Constantino
Charismatic Episcopal church
4900 Brengle Avenue
Orlando, Florida 32808

The Rt. Rev. Walter B. Conway
330 Milwee Street
Houston, Texas 77092

The Most Rev. David Cooper
Spanish Orthodox Church and EACS
18838 Roscoe Blvd.
Northridge, CA 91324-4557
(818) 773-7309
davidcooper7@prodigy.net

-D-

The Most Rev. Daniel of Mount Carmel
Orthodox Church
1750 Kalakaua Avenue, # 103-183
Honolulu, HI 96826-3795
Phone (808) 561-6010

The Rt. Rev. Danylo
Ukrainian Autocephalous Orthodox Church
Soboropravna
1416-57th Street
Cleveland, OH 44102

The Rt. Rev. Michael B. Davidson
Charismatic Episcopal Church
728 North Stevenson
Olathe, Kansas 66061

The Most Rev. C. Truman Davis
400 Usery Pass Road North
Mesa, AZ 87207

The Most Rev. Craig M. Davis
Old Catholic Orthodox Church
590-M West Main Street
Hagerstown, IN 55411

The Rt. Rev. John Dee
1601 Newton Avenue
Minneapolis, MN 55411

The Rt. Rev. Paul Deiderich
Western Orthodox Church in America
9 Hawthorne Place #10M
Boston, MA 02114

The Rt. Rev. José M. Delgado
Episcopal Missionary Church
RR 2, Buzon 6801
Manati, PR 00674

The Most Rev. Francis E. Denninson
648 Roberto Avenue
Santa Barbara, CA 93109

The Most Rev. Ken Denski
Old Catholic Church-Mathew Succession
495 Burgundy Drive
Southampton, PA 18966
rev.ken@verizon.net

Directory of Autocephalous Bishops

The Most Rev. Miguel DeSota
Western Orthodox Church of America
5262 Ellenwood Place
Los Angeles, CA 90041

The Most Rev. Timothy A. DeTraglia
Christ the Light American Catholic Church
32 Fordham Court
Albany, NY 12209-1132

The Most Rev. Edwin DeVoy
Catholic Charismatic Church
256 Higby Road
New Hartford, NY 13413

The Most Rev. David Dismas
Diocese of Rumney Marsh
165 Garfield Avenue
Chelsea, MA 02150-1319

The Most Rev. Robert M. Dittler
The White Robed Benedictines
P.O. Box 27536
San Francisco, CA 94127

The Most Rev. David Dobek
Holy Orthodox Church of Jesus the Christ
414 Bentley Place
Tucker, GA 30084

The Most Rev. Daniel L. Dolan
Traditional Roman Catholic
4900 Rialto Road
West Chester, Ohio 45069-2927

The Rt. Rev. William Downey
Liberal Catholic Church
1206 Ayers Avenue
Ojai, CA 93023

The Most Rev. David J. Doyle
The Independent Evangelical Catholic
Church in America
P.O. Box 20744
Albuquerque, NM 87154-0744

The Most Rev. Athanaois Du Bois
Western Rite Orthodox Church
220 Montoya
Taos, New Mexico 87571
Phone: (505) 751-0877
e-mail repairthebreach@ziabet.com

The Most Rev. Howard Dugan
Catholic Apostolic Church of Antioch-
  Malabar Rite
330 Madison Drive
Mt. Shasta, CA 96067

Directory of Autocephalous Bishops

The Most Rev. Raymond Dumas
10931 Circle Pine Road
North Fort Myers, Florida 33903-9006

-E-

The Rt. Rev. Joseph Eaton
525 Airport Blvd., Space #33
Watsonville, CA 95076-2031

The Most Rev. Benjamin C. Eckhardt
The Free Protestant Episcopal Church
430 Elizabeth Street
London, Ontario N5W 3R7
Canada

The Rt. Rev. Elias
Independent Greek Orthodox Church of the
   US
1668 Bush Street
San Francisco, CA 94109

The Most Rev. Elijah
Catholic Apostolic Church at Davis
921 W. 8th Street
Davis, CA 95616-3407

Directory of Autocephalous Bishops

The Most Rev. Bishop Emanuel
The Hellenic Christian Orthodox Church of
  the Diaspora
8893 Rue Saint-Hubert
Montréal, Québec H2M 2K8
Canada
Phone 514-384-6391
e-mail bishop emanuel@orthodxox.com

The Most Rev. Enoch
1133 East Olive
Fresno, CA 93728

The Most Rev. Anthony Epaphras
P.O. Box 3374
Manchester, NH 03105

-F-

The Most Rev. Francis P. Facione
The North American Old Roman Catholic
   Church (Ultrajectine Tradition)
7103 Austinwood Road
Louisville, KY 40214
Orcb1@aol.com

The Rt. Rev. Benjamin Fama
1347 Glenthorpe Drive
Diamond Bar, CA 91789
(909) 861-6628

The Most Rev. Anthony Farr
Latin Rite Catholic Church
2905 W. Yakima Ave.
Yakima, WA 98902
(509) 249-8466
gincio@aol.com

The Most Rev. Gary Carson Ferrone
Privada Andrade #102
Barrio San Marco,
Aguascalientes 20070
México
(52449) 146-5215

The Rt. Rev. Frederick G. Fick
Charismatic Episcopal Church
2225 W. Auburn Road
Rochester Hills, MI 48309

The Rt. Rev. Henry C. Filter, Jr.
Southern Episcopal Church
400 Second Avenue NE, #23
St. Petersburg, Florida 33701

The Most Rev. Christopher W. Fitzpatrick
The Western Orthodox Church in America
P.O. Box 66332
Seattle, WA 98166

The Most Rev. Edward J. Ford
North American Old Roman Catholic Church
200 Emerson Street
South Boston, MA 02127

The Most Rev. Gregory A. Francisco
Anglican Catholic Communion USA
4440 Woodruff Court
Evans, Georgia 30809
(706) 860-1402
laurengreg@aol.com

The Most Rev. George Freibott
P.O. Box 502
Nordman, ID 83880

The Rt. Rev. Charles George Fry
The Southern Episcopal Church
158 W. Union Street
Circleville, OH 43113
(740) 474-8445

The Most Rev. Robert T. Fuentes
Old Catholic Diocese of Napa
110 Pau Court
Fairfield, CA 94534

-G-

The Most Rev. Bishop Gabriel
Orthodox Church of the West
14775 US Highway 12
Adrian, MI 49230

The Most Rev. Paul Garland
Orthodox Church of Canada
367 Hazletville Road
Harty, DE 19953-2177

The Rt. Rev. Denis Garrison
201 Shepperd Road, Unit 2
Monkton, MD 21111

The Most Rev. Earl Gasquoine
Old Catholic Church in America
409 North Lexington Parkway
Deforest, WI 53532

The Rt. Rev. Wayne W. Gau
The Celtic Ecumenical Church
1666 St. Louis Drive
Honolulu HI 96816-1923
(808) 737-5654

The Most Rev. Richard Gauthier
Old Roman Catholic Church
37 Middle Drive
Weedsport, NY 13166-3140

The Rt. Rev. Walter A. Gerth
The Anglican Missionary Diocese of Texas
   Inc.
200 McGee Drive
Fort Worth, Texas 76114-4346

The Most Rev. David Gillman
United Independent Catholic Church
2717 Driftwood Drive
Mesquite, Texas 75150

The Most Rev. Dan Gincig
The American Old Catholic Church
14100 East Jewell Avenue #1
Aurora, CO 80012

Directory of Autocephalous Bishops

The Most Rev. James P. Gnat
Polish National Catholic Church
166 Pearl Street
Manchester, NH 03104

The Most Rev. Hector R. Gonzales
The Confraternity of Christian Doctrine of
    Pius X
469 Grand Street
Brooklyn, NY 11211

The Rt. Rev. Peter W. Goodrich
Independent Anglican Church-Canada Synod
18 Harvey Street
Cambridge, Ontario N3C 1N6
Canada

The Rt. Rev. Anthony G. Granitz
The Old Roman Catholic Traditional Rite
    Church
P.O. Box 49
Manhattan, Illinois 60642

The Most Rev. W. Grassman
Orthodox Catholic Church
7990 E. Snyder Road, Apt. 20104
Tucson, Arizona 85750-9043

The Rt. Rev. Ronald L. Greeson
Holy Catholic Church-Anglican Rite
3130 North Grand East
Springfield, IL 62702-4515

The Most Rev. Joseph A. Grenier
Celtic Christian Church
P.O. Box 299
Canadensis, PA 18325
(570) 595-7950

The Most Rev. Herbert Groce, Jr.
Anglican Rite Synod in Americas
875 Berkshire Valley Road
Wharton, NJ 07885-1525

The Most Rev. Walter H. Grundorf
The Anglican Province of North America
230 Robin Road
Altamonte Springs, Florida 32701
Springfield, IL 62702-4515

The Most Rev. Robert M. Gubala
The Old Catholic church in the United States
142 Progress Street
Pawtucket, RI 02860

The Most Rev. Richard Gundrey
The Catholic Apostolic Church of Antioch-
  Malabar Rite
111 W. Cordova Road
Santa Fe, NM 87505
(505) 988-4244

The Most Rev. David Guthmiller
Holy Ecumenical Anglican, Catholic Church
  of the Americas
Bldg. 17, Apt. 8
Lumberton, NJ 08048

The Most Rev. Colin J. Guthrie
Holy Orthodox Catholic Church
2249 Florence Street
Aurora, CO 80010-1120

-H-

The Rt. Rev. Robert E. Halliwell II
Independent Anglican Church
4050 Katella Ave., Suite 101
Los Alamitos, CA 90720-3405

The Rt. Rev. John M. Hammers
United Episcopal Church of North America
2340 N. 155th Street
Seattle, WA 98133

The Most Rev. Glen E. Hammett
Christ's Worldwide Apostolic Catholic
    Church
816 SW 2001
HC 71, Box 5623
Andrews, TX 79714

The Rt. Rev. G. Raymond Hanlan
The Anglican Church of America
740 Northwest 43rd Avenue
Plantation, FL 33317

Directory of Autocephalous Bishops

The Most Rev. B. P. Haralampos
The Russian True Orthodox Church
7034 Woodward Ave.
Dallas, Texas 75227
(214) 381-2294
bpharalampos@aol.com

The Most Rev. Lawrence J. Harms
The American Catholic Church in the U.S.
P.O. Box 119
Frederic, MD 21705-0119

The Most Rev. Robert C. Harvey
The Anglican Diocese of the Southwest
1845 Bedfordshire Drive
Decatur, GA 30033

The Most Rev. Wayne M. Hay
Orthodox Church of the Far Isles
260 Lauer Road
Poughkeepsie, NY 12603
Wmoorehay@yahoo.com

The Most Rev. Michael Hembree
Christ Catholic Orthodox Church
1322 Kensinger Place
Panama City, Florida 32401

The Rt. Rev. John A. Herzog
American Anglican Church
680 Albany Post Road
Briarcliff Manor, New York 10510

The Most Rev. James H. Hess
The Apostolic Christian Church
2410 Derry Street
Harrisburg, PA 17111-1141
(717) 564-9407

The Most Rev. John Hesson
Independent 1520 South Delaware Street
Paulsboro, NJ 08066

The Rt. Rev. Peter E. Hickman
The Ecumenical Old Catholic Communities
5824 W. Town and Country Road, Suite 14
Orange, CA 92868-4615
(714) 647-1770
stmattchur@aol.com

The Most Rev. John Higgins
The Church of St. Joseph
2307 South Laramie St.
Cicero, IL 60650

The Rt. Rev. Stephan A. Hoeller
Ecclesia Gnostica
3363 Glendale Blvd.
Los Angeles, CA 90039
(323) 467-2685
www.gnosis.org

The Most Rev. Ollie D. Hollis, Jr.
The Autocephalous Orthodox Church
P.O. Box 618
Grande Isle, LA 70358
(504) 628-1630

The Most Rev. John Holloway
Charismatic Episcopal Church
P. O. Box 10
Thomaston, GA 30286

The Rt. Rev. Jack E. Holman
Old Catholic Church of Utrecht
Mathew Secession
22531 August Leaf Drive
Tomball, Texas 77375

The Most Rev. S. Scott Holmes
The Anglican Church of America
482 Southbridge Street Suite 222
Auburn, MA 01501-2468

The Most Rev. Dales Howard
Charismatic Episcopal Church
8057 Arlington Expressway
Jacksonville, Florida 32211

The Most Rev. George A. Hyde
Autocephalous Orthodox Catholic Church of
   America
1305 Indian Rocks Road
Belleair, FL 33756-1057
Gahbelleair@earthlink.net

The Rt. Rev. David Hustwick
United Episcopal Church of North America
604 S. Hanover St.
Hastings, Michigan 49053
(269) 948-9327

-I-

The Most Rev. Charles Ingram
The Apostolic Orthodox Catholic church
P.O. Box 1834
Glendora, CA 91740

The Most Rev. Richard J. Ingram
Apostolic Orthodox Catholic Church
3615 Arizona Street #C
Lake Stanton, IN 46405-3121

The Rt. Rev. Jack Isbell
The United Ecumenical Catholic Church
1519 Nu'uanu Ave.
Box 76
Honolulu, HI 96817

The Most Rev. Elijah B. Israel
Saint Nikolas Ashram
P.O. Box 76
Cosmopolis, WA 98537-0076

The Most Rev. Iziaslav
The Byelorussian Autocephalic Orthodox
  Church
401 Atlantic Ave.
Brooklyn, NY 11217-1702

-J-

The Most Rev. George M. Jachimiczk
Eastern Orthodox Catholic Church
P.O. Box 15302
San Antonio, TX 78212-8502

The Rt. Rev. Roger B. Jessup
The Anglican Orthodox Church
323 Walnut Street
P.O. B 128
Statesville, NC 28687-0128

The Rt. Rev. C. Allen Jimenez
Old Catholic Church in Louisiana Mathew
  Succession
103 Brunswick Court
New Orleans, LA 70131

The Most Rev. Josef A. Johnson
African Universal Apostolic Orthodox Com-
    munity
1519 South Garnet Street
Philadelphia, PA 19146-4627

The Most Rev. James Jolly
The Anglo-Catholic Church
240-19th Avenue
Gulfport, MS 39501-4750
(228) 863-1388

The Most Rev. Charles W. Jones
Charismatic Episcopal Church
P.O. Box 661
Selma, AL 35080

The Most Rev. Rob A. Jones
Free Episcopal Church
5824-0 Redwood Road, #E257
Oakland, CA 94619

The Most Rev. David Jones
United American Orthodox Church
1000 Lake Maurer Road
Excelsior Springs, MO 64024

The Most Rev. Bernard Jordan
Zoe Ministries
P. O. Box 270
New York, NY 10009

The Most Rev. Bishop Joseph
The Society of the Good Shepherd
Good Shepherd Manor
P. O. Box 487
Willard, MO 65781

The Rt. Rev. James R. Judd
The Heartland Old Catholic Church
1624 Luella Street N.
St. Paul, MN 55119

-K-

The Rt. Rev. Patrick Kalp
P.O. Box 1175
Cedar Lake, IN 46303

The Most Rev. Lewis Keizer
The Home Temple
P. O. Box 538
Aromas, CA 95004

The Most Rev. Raymond F. Kelly
The Catholic Apostolic Church in North
   America
12017 Cheviot Drive
Herndon, VA 20170

The Most Rev. Allan A. Kelly
4083 Cervato Way
Santa Barbara, CA 93111

The Most Rev. Clarence Kelly
8 Pond Place
Oyster Bay Cove
Long Island, NY 11771

The Most Rev. Marc Kepler
American Orthodox Ministries/EOCCA
6071 Gifford Drive
Brooklyn, OH 44144-3459

The Most Rev. Douglas Kessler
Charismatic Episcopal Church
107 West Marquita
San Clemente, CA 92672

The Most Rev. Jerry A. King
The Mexican National Catholic Church
P.O. Box 1211275
Fort Worth, Texas 76121

The Most Rev. Patrick H. King
The Old Roman Catholic Church in North
    America
355-30th Street
San Francisco, CA 94131

The Most Rev. Michael D. Kirkland
Holy Orthodox Catholic Patriarchate of
    America
P.O. Box 687
New Albany, OH 43054

The Most Rev. Steven A. Kochones
American Orthodox Catholic Church
5824 La Solana Drive
Altadena, CA 91001

The Most Rev. David M. Kocka
Ecumenical Catholic Church
995 Beech Road. S. E.
Laconia, IN 47135

The Rt. Rev. Lawrence K. Kohlman
Archdiocese of the Most Precious Blood
4525 E. 19th Avenue
Denver, CO 80220
(303) 668-2154

The Most Rev. Floyd A. Kortenhof
The Old Roman Catholic Church-English
    Rite
1722 N. 79th Ave.
Elmwood Park, IL 60607
(708) 583-0334

Directory of Autocephalous Bishops

The Most Rev. Cliff Kroski
5824 Campbell Street
Kansas City, MO 64131

The Rt. Rev. Edmund Kubiak, Jr.
Orthodox Catholic Church of America
9705 W. Main St.
Belleville, IL 62223

The Most Rev. Eugene Kyle
Asatru Orthodox Fellowship Church
50 Barbour Street
Gloucester, OH 45732-1237

-L-

The Most Rev. Claude Laghi
58 Waller Street
San Francisco, CA 94102

The Rt. Rev. James F. Lagona
Western Rite Orthodox Catholic Church in
  the U.S. of America
82 Saranac Ave.
Buffalo, NY 14216-2429

The Most Rev. Dereck Lang
Church of Utrecht in America
2103 South Portland St.
Los Angeles, CA 90007

The Rt. Rev, George Langberg
Anglican Church in America
616 Eagle Valley Road
Tuxedo, New York 10987

The Rt. Alfred L. Lankenau
Orthodox Catholic Church of America
208 Kessler Blvd. E. Dr.
Indianapolis, IN 46220-2522

The Most Rev. Geoffrey D. Lantz
1511 W. Birchwood Ave. Apt. F
Chicago, Illinois 60626-1731

The Rt. Rev. Laplante
St. Raphael's Old Catholic Church
715 East 51st Ave.
Vancouver, British Columbia V5X 2E1
Canada

The Rt. Rev. Bruce D. LeBlanc
Transformational Catholic Church
P.O. Box 192
East Moline, IL. 61244-0192

The Rt. Rev. Edward Leeman
420 Confer Drive
Forked River, NJ 08731

The Most Rev. Charles M. Leigh
Apostolic Catholic Church
7837 Helen Avenue
Tampa, FL 33604
(813) 238-6060

The Rt. Rev. Leland
American Orthodox Catholic Church
722 Cedar Point Blvd. #1
Cedar Point, NC 25854
(252) 622-0449

The Rt. Rev. Charles R. Lillie
The American Catholic Church
212 Northwest Holms Blvd
Fort Walton Beach, Florida 32548

The Most Rev. Richard Lipka
Charismatic Episcopal Church
11021 Worcester Highway
Berlin, MD 21811

The Most Rev. Elic D. Llewellyn
The Free Sacramentalist Communion
26616-170th Ave. SE
Covington, WA 98042

The Most Rev. José R. López-Gaston
412 Bermudad Drive SE
Rio Rancho, NM 87124-3803
(505) 896-3622

Directory of Autocephalous Bishops

The Most Rev. John S. Lula
806 S. Espanola Street
Las Cruces, NM 88001-3936

The Rt. Rev. James Lynch
616 Lindsay Place
Knoxville, TN 37919

-*M*-

The Most Rev. Joseph Macek
546 Ashley Road
Newark, NY 13811

The Most Rev. Paget E. Mack
The Orthodox Church of St. Benedict the
   Moor
P.O. Box 17034
Brooklyn, NY 11217

The Most Rev. Ivan B. MacKillop
The Church of the Culdees
120 North 5th Street
Springfield, OR 97477

The Most Rev. Maelruain
Celtic Orthodox Christian Church
P. O. Box 72102
Akron, OH 44372

The Rt. Rev. Joseph A. Mahon
Charismatic Episcopal Church
P. O. Box 36280
Denver, CO 80236-1615

The Most Rev. John C. Maier
Old Catholic Order of Christ the King
489 Jasmine Street
Laguna Beach, CA 92651-1615
(949) 494-0679

The Most Rev. Vladyka Makarios
Ukrainian Orthodox Church-Kyivan Patriarchate
3011 Roe Drive
Houston, TX 77087

The Rt. Rev. Milton C. Mallkin
Independent Catholic-Syro-Chaldean Rite
400 E. 56th Street
New York, NY 10022-4147

The Rt. Rev. James J. Mannion
The Autocephalous Orthodox Church
P.O. Box 91653
Cleveland, OH 33101-3653

The Most Rev. Kenneth Mardian
Charismatic Catholic Church
5021 Abaran Way
Buena Park, CA 90621

The Most Rev. Markus I
The Byzantine Catholic Church, Inc.
P.O. Box 3682
Los Angeles, CA 90078-36821

The Rt. Rev. Michael D. Marshall
7561 Center Ave. #49
Huntington Beach, CA 92647

The Most Rev. Richard McCall
The Orthodox Church of America
3333 Blue Hill Road
Rogers, AR 72758

The Most Rev. Charles R. McCarthy
3078 Secane Place
Philadelphia, PA 19154-1315

The Rt. Rev. Daniel McCarthy
34334 Amesbury Road
Los Angeles, CA 90027

The Rt. Rev. Frank McCloskey
American Old Catholic Church
10860 Dogwood Drive
Stockton, AL 36579

The Most Rev. Maurice McCormick
Independent Old Catholic Church of America
8701 Brittany Drive
Louisville, KY 40220
(502) 493-8815
mauricejoann@aol.com

The Rt. Rev. Thomas McCourt
The Anglican-Independent Canada Synod
19 Lynn Road
Scarborough, Ontario M1N 2A2
Canada

The Rt. Rev. R. S. McGinnis, Jr.
Liberal Catholic Church
3417 Main Ave.
Kenner, LA 70062

The Rt. Rev. Ivan McKellop-Fritts
The Church of the Culdees
2665 C Street
Springfield, OR 06468-0283

The Most Rev. Robert McKenna
Independent-Traditional Dominican Rite
15 Pepper Street
Monroe, CT 06468-0283

The Most Rev. Scott McLaughlin
The Orthodox Anglican Communion
464 N. County Home Road
Lexington, NC 27292
(336) 236-9565
abpmclaughlin@orthodoanglican.net

The Rt. Rev. Robert McLawhorn
The Diocese of St. Paul
5721-44th Avenue South
Minneapolis, MN 55417

The Most Rev. Richard R. Melli
20253 Twin Oaks Road
Spring Hill, Florida 34610
Trad@bellsouth.net

Directory of Autocephalous Bishops

The Rt. Rev. James Meola
Independent Old Catholic Church of America
9 Abaco Street
Toms River, NJ –08753-3736
(722) 286-5604

The Rt. Rev. Bavani M. Mercado
Philippine Independent Catholic Church
581 Parwood Drive
San Diego, CA 92139

The Most Rev. Jack L. Mette
209 East Hammond Street
Roswell, NM 88203
(505) 627-3385

The Most Rev. Donald Miles
Charismatic Episcopal church
8005 Vaughn Mill Road
Louisville, KY 40228

The Most Rev. Mark I. Miller
The Byzantine Catholic Church, Inc.
P.O. Box 3682
Los Angeles, CA 90078-3682
(818) 594-0662
bcc_patriarchal_see@usa.com

The Most Rev. Michael Milner
International Free Catholic Communion
P.O. Box 3454
Clearwater, FL 33767

The Most Rev. C.H. Miner
The Orthodox Community of St. James the
    Just
1903 Baylor
Richardson, TX 75081

The Most Rev. Richard A. Monahan
North American Old Roman Catholic Church
79 Pine Hill Road
Carolina, RI 02812-1102

The Most Rev. Benton W. Montgomery
Community of Catholic Churches
1112 Steuban Street
Utica, New York 13501
(315) 735-2138

The Most Rev. Bernardo Morales
United Catholic Church
6315 Bass Highway
P.O. Box 702192
St. Cloud, FL 34771

Directory of Autocephalous Bishops

The Rt. Rev. J. B. Morgan
612 Sweetgum Ave.
Oklahoma City OK 73127-6238

The Rt. Rev. Charles E. Morley
Traditional Protestant Episcopal Church
P.O. Box 916
Point Clear, AL 36564

The Most Rev. Joseph R. Morse
Anglican Province of Christ the King
6013 Lawton Ave.
Oakland, CA 94618

The Rt. Rev. Robert S. Morse
Diocese of Christ the King
P.O. Box 40020
Berkley, CA 94704

The Most Rev. Sherman Mosley
Old Catholic Church of America
22 Stockton Lane
Egg Harbor Township
New Jersey 08234
(609) 646-6440
bishopmosley@aol.com

The Most Rev. Donald W. Mullan
Christ Catholic Church International
6190 Barker St.
Niagara Falls. Ontario L2G 1Y4
Canada

The Rt. Rev. S. Patrick Murphy
Episcopal Missionary Church
2201 Outlook Drive
Houston, Texas 77034

The Rt. Rev. Steven S. Murrell
Anglican Diocese of the Holy Spirit
208 Shady Square
Galax, VA 24333-6026

The Rt. Rev. Kenneth Myers
Charismatic Episcopal Church
P.O. Box 1281
Sherman, Texas 75091

-N-

The Most Rev. Joseph E. Neth
Liberal Catholic Church International
1736 Holly Oaks Ravine Drive
Jacksonville, FL 32225

The Most Rev. Mark E. Newman
Catholic Apostolic Church of Antioch-
    Malabar Rite
12455 N. Columbine Drive
Phoenix, AZ 85029

The Most Rev. Floyd W. Newman
Messianic Church in America
P.O. Box 309
Maple Falls, WA 98266-9999

The Rt. Rev. Nikon
American Orthodox Catholic Church
P.O. Box 479
Sudan, Texas 79371

The Rt. Rev. Robert Niznik
6616-28th Street South
Saint Petersburg, Florida 33712-5502

The Most Rev. Robert Norton
Old Catholic Church in North America
326 Hoover Ave.
Bloomfield, NJ 07003

The Most Rev. Nowlan
Genesis International
316 Hullet Street
Long Beach, CA 90805

The Rt. Rev. Edgard S. Nutt
Episcopal Missionary Church
55 Woodland Drive
Old Saybrook CT 06472

-O-

The Most Rev. Robert Ostlie
The Western Orthodox Church
3644 Clinton Ave. South
Minneapolis, MN 55409-1348
rostlie951@msn.com

-P-

The Rt. Rev. Ron Pace
Diocese of the Abiding Presence
1411 Nursery Road
Clearwater, FL 33756

The Most Rev. Rick Painter
Charismatic Episcopal Church
P. O. Box 43077
Phoenix, AZ 85080

The Most Rev. Mario-Arturo Palomino
Holy Ecumenical Anglican Catholic Church
   of the Americas
358 Madison Ave,
Paterson, NJ 07524

The Rev. John Parnel
The Mexican National Catholic Church
270 Bayon Street
Fort Worth, Texas 76114

The Most Rev. Norman Parr
The Old Catholic Church in America
11312 N. 100 E
Alexander, IN 46001

The Most Rev. Luigi de Jesus Pasquale
Holy Ukrainian Autocephalic Orthodox
    Church in Exile
103 Evergreen Street
West Babylon, NY 11704

The Rt. Rev. Sirhij K. Pastukhiv
Holy Ukrainian Autocephalic Orthodox
    Church in Exile
103 Evergreen Street
West Babylon, NY 11704

The Most Rev. Martin J. Patton
Old Catholic Church in North America
9200 Montgomery Road 12A
Montgomery, Ohio 45242

The Most Rev. Timothy B. Paul
Western Rite Orthodox Catholic Church
P.O. Box 2302
Springfield, MA 01101

The Rt. Rev. Thaddeus Peplowski
5776 Broadway
Lancaster, NY 14086-2359

The Most Rev. Eurico Peppe
The Apostolic Church of Jerusalem
P.O. Box 68
Holder, Florida 34486-2359

The Most Rev. John H. Perry-Hooker
Anglican Church of America
Doe Corner
Newbury, VT 05051-0208

The Most Rev. Petros
American Orthodox Catholic Church
P.O. Box 39535
Los Angeles, CA 90039-0535

The Most Rev. Stephen Pfleiderer
The Celtic Orthodox Old Catholic Church
3004 NW 32nd Street
Oklahoma City, OK 73112-6916

The Most Rev. Mark A. Pivarunas
Traditional Roman Catholic church
7745 Military Ave.
Omaha, NE 68134

The Most Rev. Bernard Price
Mar Thomas Orthodox Church
1301 East Ave. #377
Lancaster, PA 93535-2155
The Most Rev. Karl Pruter
Christ Catholic Church
405 Kentling Road
P.O. Box 63
Highlandville, MO 65669

The Most Rev. Clement Poling
Ancient Orthodox Catholic Church
101 Lyles Miles
Pennsboro, WV
(304) 659-26415

The Most Rev. Michael Pugin
Catholic Apostolic Church in North America
1406 Coolridge Street
Hollywood, FL 33020-2555

The Most Rev. Mark Pultarak
American Orthodox Catholic Church
460 S. Massey Street
Watertown, NY 13601

-Q-

The Rt. Rev. Bill Quinlan
Reformed Catholic Church
3359 Swans Road, NE
Newark, OH 43055
(740) 345-0857
QnlBi@aol..com

-R-

The Most Rev. Joseph J. Raffaele
American Orthodox Catholic Church
318 Waverly Ave.
Medford, NY 11763

The Most Rev. John J. Rankin
The Church of the Divine Presence
One South Plaza Ste.151
Tahlequah, OK 74464

The Most Rev. Stephen C. Reber
United Episcopal Church of North America
614 Pebblestone Court
Statesville, NC 28677
(704) 871-0272

The Most Rev. Adrian R. Ravarour
American Catholic Church
P.O. Box 39828
Los Angeles, CA 90039-0828

The Most Rev. John J. Rankin
The Church of the Divine Presence
One South Plaza, Ste. 151
Tahlequah, OK 74464

The Most Rev. Stephen C. Reber
United Episcopal Church of North America
614 Pebblestone Court
Statesville, NC 28677

The Most Rev. John Reeves
United Independent Catholic Church
1603 Old Creal Springs Road
Marion, IL 62959-6456

The Most Rev. Angelo Ricci
Apostolic Orthodox Catholic Church
37 Sheppee School House Road
Foster, RI 02825

The Most Rev. Gerald Richards
Lamb of God Apostolic Independent Catholic
    Church
677 Stable Gate Lane
Florence, KY 41042

The Most Rev. Rodney Rickard
United Catholic Church
204 Panamint Drive
Antioch, TN 37013

The Most Rev. John A. Rinaldi
The Free Catholic church
1010 University Ave. #175
San Diego, CA 92103

The Rt. Rev. Peter Riola
Communion of Anglican Churches
23198 Jivaro St. NW
St. Francis, MN 55070
(763) 213-8073
stalcuin@aol.com

The Most Rev. Perry Rist
American Catholic Church
1498 Sunshine Drive
Concord, CA 94520-4069

The Most Rev. Robert Ritorto
United Independent Catholic Church
P. O. Box 2956
Zanesville, OH 43702-2956

The Rt. Rev. Jerome Robben
Christ Catholic Church International
P. O. Box 5676
Chesterfield, MO 63006-0566

The Most Rev. William O. Roberts
Liberal Catholic Church International
2930 E. Sable Circle
Margate, Florida 33063
Roberts208@bellsouth.net

The Rt. Rev. Emile F. Rodrigues V. Fairfield
The Mexican National Catholic Church
4011 Brooklyn Ave.
East Los Angeles, CA 90022

The Rt. Rev. Christopher Rogers
4428 Moorpark Way
North Hollywood, CA 91602-2424

The Most Rev. Frederic M. Rothermel
Old Roman Catholic Church
1330 N. 38 Drive
Phoenix, AZ 85009-3244

The Most Rev. Richard G. Roy
The National Catholic Church of America
166 Jay Street
Albany, NY 12210

Directory of Autocephalous Bishops

The Most Rev. Joseph Royer
Orthodox Church of Canada
5824-118 Avenue
Edmonton, Alberta T5W 1E4
Canada

The Rt. Rev. Arthur C. Ruslow
5646 S.E. 28th Street
Ocala, Florida 32670

The Most Rev. Emigidius J. Ryzy
The American World Patriarchs
19 Aqueduct Street
Ossining, New York 10562

-S-

The Most Rev. John F. Saccone
Anglican Catholic Byzantine Orthodox
  Church
329 Hillview Ave.
Syracuse, NY 13207

The Most Rev. Donald Saint-Peters
6329 East 55th Place
Indianapolis, IN 46266

The Most Rev. Paul R. Sale
Church of the Fisherman-Orthodox Catholic
  Church
3047 Nevada Avenue
El Monte, CA 91731

The Rt. Rev. Joseph Salm
Independent Anglican Church Canada Synod
850 Hamilton Ave.
Rockledge, Florida 32955-3508

The Rt. Rev. Roland L. Salvador
Catholic Charismatic Church of Canada
575 Wickenden Street #108
Providence, RI 02903-4454

The Most Rev. Raymond E. Sawyer
1205 Thomas Blvd.
Springdale, AR 72762

The Most Rev. Basil Schott
Byzantine Catholic Eparchy of Parma
1900 Carlton Road
Parma, FL 44134

The Most Rev. Michael V. Seneco
227 Tennessee Ave. NE
Washington, DC 20002

The Most Rev. Yaroslaw R. Sereda
The Orthodox Church of Canada
40 Odessa Blvd.
Terra Cotta, Ontario L0P 1N0
Canada

The Rt. Rev. Larry Lee Shaver
195 East 68th Place
Merrillville, IN 46410

The Most Rev. William L. Shedrick, Jr.
Old Roman African Orthodox Church International
national
4406-16 Redwood Highway #393
San Rafael, CA 94903

The Most Rev. Mark S. Shirlau
The Ecumenical Catholic Church
14801 Comet Street
Irvine, CA 92604
(949) 451-1531

The Most Rev. Perry Sills
   The Evangelical Orthodox Catholic Church
in America
1213 N. San Pedro Street
San Jose, CA 95110-1436

The Most Rev. Lee Schmidt
201 E. Carolyn Drive
Pleasant Hope, MO 65725

The Most Rev. Randolph Sly
Charismatic Episcopal Church
46797 Trailwood Place
Pontiac Falls, VA 20165

The Most Rev. Sean Small
15342 Cascade Lane
Huntington Beach, CA 92647

The Rt. Rev. Albert Smith
1205 Thomas Blvd.
Springdale, AR 72762

The Rt. Rev. Clarence T. Smith
American Anglican church
3935 Parker Road
Florissant, MO 63033

The Rt. Rev. George T. Smith
The United Catholic Church of America
P.O. Box 1000
Mt. Freedom, NJ 07970

The Rt. Rev. Lawrence J. Smith
The Liberal Catholic Church
9740 South Avers
Evergreen Park, IL 60805

The Rt. Rev. Norman (Ken) Smith
Christ Catholic Church International
76-770 Hualalai Road
Kailua-Kona, HI 96740

The Most Rev. Robert D. Smith
Christ Catholic Church International
824 Royal Oak Drive
Orlando. Florida 32809

The Rt. Rev. Juan V. Solanas
The Traditional Episcopal Diocese of St.
   James
4751 NE 6th Avenue
Ft. Lauderdale, Florida 33334-2330

The Most Rev. Francis C. Spataro
The Western Rite Vicariate (Uniate Western
   Orthodox Church
80-46 234th Street
Queens NY 11427-21116
(914) 579-0585
cil11427@mycingular.blackberry.com

The Rt. Rev. Chet Stachewicz
Orthodox Catholic Church of America
5600 Gibson Blvd. SE Apt 143
Albuquerque, NM 87108

The Most Rev. George A. Stallings, Jr.
The African American Catholic Congregation
10911 194th Street Ct. E
Graham, WA 98338-8142

The Most Rev. John M. Stanley
5068 SE Hortsman Road
Port Orchard, WA 98366-3904

The Rt. Rev. Rommie Starks
The Anglican Catholic Church
6361 North Keystone Ave
Indianapolis, IN 46220

The Rt. Rev. George D. Stenhouse
Episcopal Missionary Church
2216 Goldsmith Road
Louisville, KY 41042

The Most Rev. Stephanous
Ukrainian Autocephalous National Orthodox
118 East Fifth Ave.
Altoona, Pa 16602

The Most Rev. Peter J. Sterling
Unaffiliated/Independent
183 Main Street
Matawan, NJ 07747

The Most Rev. Rick Stone-Williams
Society of Stephan
P.O. Box 6225
Altadena, CA 91003

The Most Rev. Donald B. Stouder
The Thomas Christians
5555 Grossmont Center Drive
La Mesa, CA 91942

The Most Raymond Stroll
Celtic Orthodox Catholic Church
3004 NW 32nd Street
Oklahoma City OK 73112

The Most Rev. Steven J. Styblo
Independent Episcopal Old Catholic Church
P.O. Box 14370
Phoenix, AZ 85063

The Most Rev. Richard H. Svihus
P.O. Box 1773
Chico, CA 95925

The Most Rev. John F. Swanteck
The Polish National Catholic Church
1002 Pittston Avenue
Scranton, PA 18505

The Most Rev. Carl Swaringim
Ecumenical Catholic Church + USA
1110 Whispering Pines Drive
O'Fallon, MO 63368-6758

-T-

The Most Rev. Joseph Thaddeus
713 West Sprice #90
Deming, NM 88030

The Rt. Rev. George Theckedath
Nazrani Orthodox Mission
2270 Courtice Avenue
Ottawa, Ontario K1H 7G8
Canada

The Most Rev. Stephen Thomas
The Romano-Byzantine Orthodox Catholic
   Church
5907 Grand Avenue
Duluth, MN 55807

The Most Rev. Charles Thorp
349 Moreton Bay Lane #3
Goleta, CA 93117-6243
lechemininot@earthlink.net

The Most Rev. Timofi
The Ukrainian Orthodox church
3011 Roe Drive
Houston, Texas 77087

The Most Rev. Bishop Timothy of Duluth
Syro-Russian Orthodox Catholic Church
5907 Grand Avenue
Duluth, MN 55807
RBSOCC@juno.com

The Rt. Rev Joseph L. Tisch
The Liberal Catholic Church, Province of the
    USA
P.O Box 1117
Melbourne, FL 32902
(321) 254-0499
tischainpierre@aol.com

The Most Rev. Roberto C. Toca
The Catholic Church of the Antiochean Rite
P.O. Box 8473
Tampa, FL 33674-8473

The Rt. Rev. Jona Tolson
The Orthodox Byzantine Old Calendar Dio-
    cese of Berkeley
1671 Golden Gate Avenue #2
San Francisco, CA 94115

The Most Rev. Tooms II
The Federation of St. Thomas Christians
525 Airport Blvd. #33
Watsonville, CA 95070

The Rt. Rev. Douglas L. Trees
Chevaliers de Notre Dame (SSPX)
The Preceptory
176 Lake Ave.
Suffolk, NY 11780
(631) 584-5789
blackfridr@blackfriar.org

The Most Rev. Patrick E. Trujillo
Old Catholic Church in America
6020 Newkirk Ave.
North Bergen, NJ 07047
Poetpat@optonline.net

The Most Rev. Mathew Tux
Free Protestant Episcopal Church
1033 Adelaide N.
London, Ontario N5Y 2M8
Canada

-*U*-

The Most Rev. Charles Unger
Independent Old Catholic Church
5973 Island View Drive
Buford, GA 30851

-V-

The Most Rev. Enrique L. Valenzuela
Holy Ecumenical Anglican Catholic Church
  of the Americas
79 Butter Street
Paterson, NJ 07524

The Most Rev. Joseph Valone
North American Old Catholic Church
19230 Mallory Canyon Rd.
Salinas, CA 93907

The Rt. Rev. Frank W. Vandeventer
Christ Catholic Orthodox Church
2079 Harkness Ave.
Cincinnati, OH 45225
(513) 699-6853
fvandeventer@cinci.rr.com

The Most Rev. William C. Vannerus
The American Catholic Apostolic Church
1611 Banciforte Drive
Santa Cruz, CA 95965
The Most Rev. Anthony R. Vassallo
Christ Catholic Church
4066 Royal Lane
Dallas, Texas 75229

The Paul V. Verhaeren
Orthodox Church of the Far Isles
260 Lauer Road
Poughkeepsie, NY 12603
(845) 473-5161
pverhaeren@yahoo.com

The Most Rev. Michael E. Verra
American Catholic Church
238 Mott Street
New York, NY 11012

The Rt. Rev. Victor
American Orthodox Catholic Church
P.O. Box 477
Sudan, Texas 79371
(806) 577-4102

Directory of Autocephalous Bishops

The Rt. Rev. Louis Vides
Order of St. Francis of Assisi
P.O. Box 16194
Rochester, NY 14663

The Most Rev. Vides
Iglesia Episcopal Ascensión
10154 Mountain Ave.
Tujunga, CA 92042

The Most Rev. Dom J. Villegas
Catholic Apostolic Church in North America
259 West 19th Street, Apt. 14
New York, NY 10024

The Most Rev. Joseph Vredenberg
St. Thomas Christians
134 Dakota Street #308
Santa Cruz, CA 9560
(831) 423-4952

-W-

The Most Rev. Philip Weeks
Charismatic Episcopal Church
8057 Arlington Expressway
Jacksonville, FL 32211

The Rt. Rev. Carl L. Weschcke
Paracletian Catholic Church
P.O. Box 64386
St. Paul, MN 55164-0383

The Rt. Rev. Peter A. Wilkinson
209-25 Government Street
Victoria, British Columbia V8V 2K4
Canada

The Rt. Rev. James A. Wilkowski
The Evangelical Catholic Diocese of the
    Northwest
P.O. Box 178388
Chicago, IL 60617

The Most Rev. Robert Williams
Old Catholic Church in America
19905 South 3rd Street
Austin, Texas 78704

The Rt. Rev. William Wise
The Independent Catholic Church
P.O. Box 2546
Eugene, OR 97402

The Most Rev. Bronislaw L. Wojdyla
1317 North Ashland Ave
Chicago, Illinois 60622

The Most Rev. Jerry Wood
United Independent Catholic Church
1525 E. Glenn Avenue
Springfield, Illinois 62703

The Most Rev. D. Worley
American Orthodox Catholic Church
105 Washington Street Apt 306
Watertown, NY 13601

The Rt. Rev. Jackson Worsham
The Traditional Protestant Episcopal Church
112 Pheasant Run
Battle Creek, MI 49015
(269) 963-2679

R.I.P.
†

The Most Rev. Michael Bent
The Most Rev. Charles A. Browne
The Most Rev. David Javore
The Rt. Rev. Herman Keck, Jr.
The Rt. Archimandrite Mark (Gielow)
The Rt. Rev. L. Mac McFerran
The Rt. Rev. James O. Mote
The Rt. Rev. John-Noel Murray
The Most Rev. Anthony F. Savage

RETURN TO SENDER
†

The Most Rev. Gilbert Arnald
The Rt. Rev. Ronald L. Bair
The Most Rev. Timothy P. Bayman
The Rt. Rev. Stephen Clark
The Most Rev. Philip M. Edge
The Most Rev. Montgomery Griffith-Mair
The Most Rev. Henry F. Hegarty
The Most Rev. David A. Horsman
The Most Rev. John P. Hozvicka
The Most Rev. Donald E. Hugh
The Most Rev. Roland D. Jacques
The Most Rev. George Le Mesurier
The Most Rev. Vince Lavieri
The Rt. Rev. Joseph Lempel
The Most Rev. Claude Light
The Most Rev. David Moody
The Rt. Rev. Robert M. Nemkovich
The Rt. Rev. Jerry L. Ogles
The Most Rev. Michael Owen

The Most Rev. Edward C. Paync
The Most Rev. Michael G. Newsmith
The Most Rev. Karl Rodig
The Most Rev. Jorge Rodriquez-Villa
The Most Rev. Jon Ryner
The Most Rev. Richard Saint-John
The Most Rev. Fred Sansone
The Most Rev. F. Wilson Sehorn
The Most Rev. David E. Strong
The Most Rev. Vladimer Sergius II
The Rt. Rev. Randolph J. Sykes
The Rt. Rev. Clay Teppenpaw
The Most Rev. Pierre Testart
The Most Rev. Theodore
The Rt. Rev. Alfred Woolcock
The Most Rev. Walter C. Wood, Jr.
The Rt. Rev. Charles E. Worrell, Sr.

Directory of Autocephalous Bishops

ABOUT THE EDITOR
✝

BISHOP KARL PRÜTER was born in 1920 in Poughkeepsie, New York. Following high school there he completed undergraduate work at Boston's Northeastern University, and then earned his master's degree in divinity at the Lutheran Theological Seminary in Philadelphia. After starting his ecclesiastical career as a congregational minister, he wrote two books, the second of which, *Neo-Congregationalism*, was later revised to include a chapter relating the personal sojourn that brought him to the Old Catholic Movement.

In 1967 Bishop Prüter was consecrated bishop of Christ Catholic Church, and the church, under his leadership, has significantly influenced the entire Old Catholic Movement. He served as presiding bishop of Christ Catholic Church from 1967 to June 1991, when he then became suffragan bishop in order to have more time to devote to spiritual writing and to promoting the retreat movement. Throughout his work in the church, Bishop Prüter has conducted literally hundreds of retreats for both Protestant and Catholic groups.

Along with having written scores of religious pamphlets, Bishop Prüter has also authored eight books, among them *The Teachings of the Great Mystics, A History of the Old Catholic Church, The Priest's Handbook*, and, most recently, *One Day with God* (Borgo Press, 1991), a self-instructional guide to spiritual retreats. He currently resides in Springfield, Missouri, where he serves the Cathedral of the Prince of Peace in Highlandville, which is listed in the *Guinness Book of World Records* as the planet's smallest cathedral, measuring 14 x 17 feet and seating fifteen people.

www.ingramcontent.com/pod-product-compliance
Lightning Source LLC
LaVergne TN
LVHW011213080426
835508LV00007B/770